CHESS FOR BE

A Clear And Complete Guide To Easily Learn

How To Play Chess With Basic Tactics,

Strategies, And Tips For Beginners

By

Larry Lawrenson Smith

Please consult a licensed professional before attempting any techniques outlined in this book.

By reading this document, the reader agrees that under no circumstances is the author responsible for any losses, direct or indirect, which are incurred as a result of the use of information contained within this document, including, but not limited to, — errors, omissions, or inaccuracies.

TABLE OF CONTENTS

INTRODUCTION 1

HISTORY OF CHESS 2

REASONS WHY YOU SHOULD PLAY CHESS 5

CHAPTER 1: THE CHESSBOARD AND THE PIECES 7

ALL ABOUT CHESS PIECES.................................... 8

POINT VALUES OF EACH PIECE 11

PLAYING THE GAME.. 12

CHAPTER 2: THE STARTING POSITION........................... 17

HOW THE PIECES MOVE....................................... 19

The Pawn 20

The Bishop 23

The Knight 24

The Queen...26

The King 28

CAPTURING.. 29

SPECIAL MOVES 31

En Passant 31

Pawn Promotion 33

Castling 34

CHAPTER 3: CHESS NOTATION 38

CHAPTER 4: BASIC OPENING STRATEGIES 42

KING'S PAWN OPENINGS 43

QUEEN'S PAWN OPENINGS 48

FLANK OPENINGS 51

CHOOSING YOUR OPENING 53

CHAPTER 5: BASIC MIDDLE GAME STRATEGIES 55

AREAS OF FOCUS IN THE MIDDLEGAME 56

CHAPTER 6: BASIC ENDGAME STRATEGIES 60

ENDGAMES WITHOUT PAWNS 62

KING AND PAWN ENDGAMES 65

KING AND KNIGHT ENDGAMES 69

KING AND BISHOP ENDGAMES 71

KING AND ROOK ENDGAMES 73

KING AND QUEEN ENDGAMES 75

ENDGAME THEORY VS REALITY 79

CHAPTER 7: CHECKMATING PATTERNS 81

ANDERSEN'S COLLEAGUE 81

ARAB NEIGHBOR 82

THE PLAYER BEHIND THE RANK 82

BISHOP AND KNIGHT OF THE MAIDANA 82

BLACKBURN'S WIFE 83

MATT FIELD 83

CORNER COUPLE 84

COSIO'S WIFE 84

SIMILAR TO BISHOP DAMIANO 84

DAMIANO'S COLLEAGUE 84

THE WIFE OF DAVID AND GOLIATH 85

SAME COLOR AS DOUBLE BISHOP 85

COLUMBOFIL COLLEAGUE 85

EPAULETTE'S SPOUSE 86

GRECO'S COLLEAGUE 86

THE WIFE IN FILE H 86

PAIR ROOK 87

THE ASSIGNMENT OF THE KING AND THE 2 BISHOPS 87

THE KING AND THE 2 KNIGHTS HAVE A PROJECT 87

LOLLY'S NEIGHBOR 87

A COLLEAGUE OF MAX LANGE 88

MURPHY'S MATE 88

OPERA COLLEAGUE 88

COMRADE PILLSBURY 89

THE SPOUSE OF THE QUEEN 89

RETI'S MATE 89

COLLEAGUE MATE 90

THE NEIGHBOR'S SLEEP 90

SWALLOW'S TAIL 90

CHAPTER 8: TACTICS **91**

BATTERY ATTACK 92

    Queen and Bishop's Battery *92*

    Queen and Rook's Battery *93*

    Queen and 2x Rooks - Battery *93*

    2x Rooks- Battery *94*

DISCOVERED ATTACK 95

DISCOVERED CHECK 96

FORK ATTACK 97

    Relative Fork Attack *98*

    Absolute Fork Attack *98*

PIN ATTACK 99

    Relative Pin Attack *99*

Absolute Pin Attack *100*

SKEWER ATTACK 101

Relative Skewer Attack *101*

Absolute Skewer Attack *102*

EVALUATING POSITIONAL ELEMENTS 104

Material Value *104*

Space *105*

Control of the Center *105*

Initiative *105*

Development *106*

King's Safety *106*

Weak Squares and Open Lines *107*

Pawn Structure *107*

EVALUATING TACTICAL ELEMENTS 108

King's Safety *108*

Overloaded Pieces *109*

Unprotected Pieces *109*

Pinned Pieces *109*

Peculiar Piece Placements *110*

CALCULATION OF VARIATIONS 110

DEVELOPING A WINNING COMBINATION 111

TESTING THE SOUNDNESS OF COMBINATIONS 111

CHAPTER 9: TIPS FOR BEGINNERS **113**

CHAPTER 10: COMMON MISTAKES TO AVOID 117

FAILING TO TAKE CHARGE OF THE CENTER 117

LEAVING YOUR KING EXPOSED 118

FAILURE TO DEVELOP YOUR CHESS PIECES 119

COPYING YOUR OPPONENT'S EVERY MOVE 120

USING YOUR QUEEN VERY EARLY 121

WASTING TEMPOS 123

BEING CLUMSY ON THE CHESSBOARD 123

TOUCHING ONE OF YOUR PIECES INADVERTENTLY 124

TOUCHING YOUR OPPONENT'S PIECES INADVERTENTLY 124

HASTENING TO MAKE A MOVE 125

CONCLUSION 126

INTRODUCTION

When many people just look at all they have to go through to learn chess game, they simply decide to give up. Nevertheless, chess remains an interesting game that anyone should learn to play and actually play for various reasons.

Often, when some people want to learn how to play chess, they don't usually know where to seek guidance. The guide is written in simple language, devoid of any form of unnecessary jargon. This is to make the learning process easy for you.

Even though this guide is for beginners, it is also recommended for people who already know how to play chess but want to improve their skills or learn new moves. The guide is simple to follow and understand—it is devoid of superfluous information.

Let's explore chess and all its amazing facets, starting with how this amazing game first began, in one of the cradles of civilization, India.

History of Chess

The precise origins of the game we now call chess remains a mystery, with historians and anthropologists still debating over the subject. However, what's generally agreed is that the earliest known ancestor of the game originated in India sometime before the 6th century CE. This early predecessor, called chaturanga, was quite different from the game we know today. A war game, chaturanga took its name from a military formation mentioned in the epic Mahabharata. The formation itself refers to four divisions within the army: infantry, cavalry, chariotry, and elephantry.

As chaturanga evolved, so did the names it was known by around 600 CE, chatrang became a growing pastime in Persia and Central Asia, where it later spread to further east, gaining recognition with different cultures, calling it different names. In Mongolia, it was called shatar, in China, xiangqi, and in Japan, shogi. Each culture brought its unique perspective to the rules of the game and the character of the pieces, but two fundamental qualities of chaturanga persisted in each variation. First, unlike in checkers, different pieces had different capabilities. Second, capturing the opponent's king was the path to victory. These qualities remain fundamental to the DNA of modern chess.

Chess reached Europe by the 10th century CE by way of expanding the Islamic Empire. When chatrang was introduced to the Arab world, it was redubbed shatranj but remained largely similar to the game's Persian variation.

The early Islamic conquests brought bloodshed to both the Levant and the Iberian Peninsula but also brought cultural and technological innovations, including shatranj. The Greeks called it zatrikion, while in Spain, it became known as ajedrez. Both cultures initially retained the Persian names given to each piece. As the game spread throughout the medieval world, the Persian word shāh ("king") gradually evolved into the English chess. The phrase "Shāh Māt!" ("The king is helpless") would likewise develop into the modern term checkmate.

Chess quickly took the European world by storm as it became so popular that at times both the church and secular authorities attempted to prohibit the games—and the gambling that often came with it. Eventually, the names of the pieces began to change to reflect the local culture. Elephants became bishops and the vazīr, or minister, became the Queen.

The game rules continued to change by 1300; an addition had been made to the rules, allowing pawns to move two squares on their first move. Later, sometime before 1500, the previously weak Queen and bishops gained new abilities to make them more useful and speed up play. Once referred to as Queen's Chess, this modified ruleset later developed into the modern standard of play by the 19th century.

Since the birth of modern competitive chess in 1851, when German-born Adolf Anderssen won the first-ever international chess tournament, the sport has exploded into a worldwide phenomenon. Countless grandmasters, men, and women hailing from dozens of countries around the world have risen to prominence throughout the decades.

In the late 20th Century, chess even became a topic of a heated political conversation. When the 1972 World Chess Championship pitted American prodigy Bobby Fischer against Russian champion Boris Spassky, both rival nations took immense interest in the match's outcome. When Fischer won the game, ending 24 years of Soviet dominance in competitive play, it was touted as a blow against the USSR itself. Later, when Fischer defied U.S. sanctions to attend an unofficial rematch against Spassky in 1992, a warrant was issued for his arrest.

Today, the Fédération Internationale des Échecs (FIDE) acts as the governing body of competitive chess worldwide. New names have come to prominence in recent years, including Hungary's Judit Polgar, widely considered the strongest female player in the game's history. The current reigning champion, Magnus Carlsen of Norway, holds the highest peak classical rating in history with a score of 2882.

Reasons Why You Should Play Chess

Better Brain Function: the mind is astounding — it is liable for our psychological exhibition, and it is the most significant organ in the human body. At the point when the mind has no incitement, the cells inside gradually kick the bucket; it's a case of "in the event that you don't utilize it, you lose it" motto, notwithstanding, chess is an instrument which gives clients a thorough mental exercise. How about we take a gander at a snappy model: to get the most profit by a physical exercise, you have to practice both the left and right sides of your body. Studies demonstrate that to play chess well, a player must create and use their mind's left side of the equator, which manages object acknowledgment, just as the correct side of the equator, which manages design acknowledgment. After some time, on account of the guidelines and methods engaged with the game, playing chess will viably practice and create not one but rather the two sides of your cerebrum. Researchers likewise guarantee that playing chess can improve mental age by as long as 14 years.

Improved Memory: researchers have demonstrated that chess helps keep Alzheimer's malady under control, which is straightforwardly identified with memory loss. There are numerous strategies and systems in chess, and a decent player should know a large portion of them, yet it isn't the situation of sitting and learning the strategies by heart. Through the span of numerous games, players build up a practically normal sentiment of when to utilize a specific system or strategy—this is the place the advantages of improved memory sparkle—players can rapidly recollect and utilize various techniques or strategies. Best of all, this advantage isn't just restricted to chess—improved memory can be seen in different everyday issues, for example, scholastic execution, obligations, duties, and so forth.

Chapter 1:

THE CHESSBOARD AND THE PIECES

Before one can start in the chess game, they should be familiar with its objective, the pieces used to play the game, and which the player can do moves.

Chess is a two-player game in which the win condition is to threaten the opposing player's King so that it won't be able to avoid getting captured (also called a checkmate). Players can eliminate the pieces of their opponents by moving their own pieces so that they can get closer to their goal.

The "game field" is a board with 8 rows and 8 columns of boxes, alternating colors that are similar to a checkered flag. Each column is designated with a letter (A to H) from left to right, while the rows are assigned with numbers (1 to 8) starting from the bottom. Rows are called **ranks**, while columns are called **files**.

The following page's image shows what a chessboard looks like and the starting position of all the pieces. It also shows the imaginary numbers and letters on the board that shows the positioning of each piece.

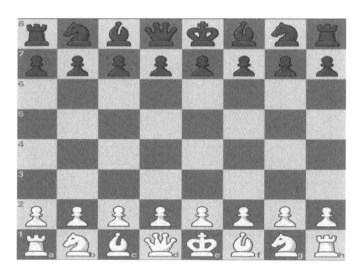

The pieces are either white or black. Players take turns making one move per turn, and the game starts with white, always making the first move.

All about Chess Pieces

The chess game is like a battlefield wherein the soldiers of each general (or player) are the pieces.

Each player is provided with 16 pieces that should be placed in their starting positions accordingly. These pieces, depending on what they are, can only be moved in a certain way, which are as follows:

- **Pawn** - Each player has 8 of these. Pawns can only move one square forward at a time except for their first move, as they can move 2 squares forward from the starting position. Pawns have a different way of capturing an opponent's pieces, as they can only eliminate opposing pieces diagonally forward one square, either to the left or to the right. Their starting positions are on the **2nd** rank for white and the **7th** rank for black.

- **Rook** – This looks like a tower and can move horizontally or vertically for any number of squares as long as those squares are not blocked. It can capture opposing pieces that are within the area of their movement range. Each player has 2 rooks. Their starting positions are the corners of the game board.

- **Knight** – This piece looks like a horse (and sometimes called as such). It can move in an L-like fashion; that is, from its initial position, the player should move it two squares either horizontally or vertically, and then move it one square to the left or right. So long as the player can draw that imaginary L when this piece moves, it is legal. The place where it should land is the square that it can capture. Because of this knight's quality, it can "jump over" other pieces as long as its landing spot is unobstructed. Players have 2 knights, and those are placed beside the rooks.

- **Bishop** – This can move any number of squares diagonally depending on the square's color where it is placed (determined by the starting position) and can capture opposing pieces in its movement range. Both players are given 2 bishops, and they start next to the knight.

- **Queen** – The Queen can move to any unobstructed square after moving diagonally, vertically, or horizontally. Players only have 1 queen at the start of the game and are placed on the square beside the bishop that corresponds to the piece's color (White's Queen occupies the light-colored square next to the bishop while Black's Queen occupies the dark-colored square).

- **King** – The king can move one square in any direction except when castling. Each player has one King, and it is placed beside the Queen.

Point Values of Each Piece

A player can have an idea of their advantage over their opponent based on their point differences.

Each piece in the game is assigned with a numerical value, and a player gets points depending on the pieces that they have captured during the game.

The point values are as follows:

- Pawn = 1 point

- Bishop and Knight = 3 points

- Rook = 5 points

- Queen = 9 points

The king has no assigned value since it cannot be captured. These point values are directly proportional to their contribution to the game. For example, since the Queen has more liberty when it comes to its moves, it has a higher value compared to other pieces that have some form of limitations.

To apply this concept, let's say that you can capture your opponent's bishop while he can capture your knight. Since both pieces have the value of 3 points, the game is not yet in any player's favor. However, if you are able to capture the opponent's rook, but he can only get a bishop, it can be seen that you now have an advantage when looking at the points of each captured piece.

Think of these point values as the power level of each side. As the game goes on, the goal is to significantly decrease your opponent's power level and ensure that yours is higher. This also implies that to analyze the game carefully, they simply need to look at how many points remain for them and their opponents.

Playing the Game

After getting to know how all your pieces work and what their strong and weak points are, you need to arrange them on the board in order to start your game. First, you need to make sure that the light-colored square is located at the bottom right corner of the players. You don't want to play on the wrong side of the board. After which, set up your pieces in the following manner:

1. Make sure you have 16 pieces complete, all having the same color.

2. Position all of your eight pawns on the second row in front of you.

3. Next, position each rook on both corners on your side of the chessboard.

4. Place one Knight beside each rook and then place a bishop next to it.

5. Then, position the Queen in one of the two remaining spaces. If your piece is light-colored, place it on the light-colored square. If it is dark-colored, then place it on the dark-colored square as well.

6. Lastly, place the King on the last space remaining. Try to check if the opposite side has a similar arrangement as yours with the Kings and Queens opposite to each other.

When everything on your board is in place, you are now ready to start your game. In playing the game chess, one must also remember the following things:

1. The player with the light-colored pieces makes the first move. They can pick any piece that is allowed for movement, pawns, and horses. The players take turns in playing, and it is not allowed to make two successive movements at any point of the game.

2. Depending on the strategy you want to use, try to position your pieces to their most useful posts. You want your pieces to be in safe and good squares in order to avoid having more pieces captured than that of the opponent.

3. Each move you make should only be done using only one hand. Also remember that you cannot move two pieces at a time except in the special move called castling.

4. In this game, there is what we call a touch-move rule, which states that you should move the piece you already touched unless if it places the King in a check. This is a basic rule in chess that is why it applies to every game, except if the players agreed beforehand not to adhere to it. In addition to this, if you touch an opponent's piece, it must then be captured if possible. If it's not, then the game continues as if it had not been touched.

5. However, if you want to adjust or align your pieces properly, you can do so without committing a touch-move by saying in advance that you are going to move a piece. Notify your opponent first so that you will not encounter any conflicts during the game.

6. The ultimate end goal of the game is to capture the King. All your strategies and movements must lead towards this goal. To emphasize it again, the King must be protected at all times because once you lose it before your opponent does, then you lose your game.

7. When moving your other pieces, try to keep track of whether each move will put your King to risk. Also, look at your opponent's every move. Do not become too relaxed at any point of the game so that you can detect threats and possible attacks by the opponent.

8. During the whole duration of the game, try as much as possible to think a step or two in advance. If you move once piece, try to think about what happens after. Does it expose the other pieces, or does it go into a position where you can play offense or defense? It is important to plot your movements with tact, proper timing, and strategy in order to increase your chances of winning the game. Take time to prepare your every movement to avoid mistakes and miscalculations.

9. The game must be conducted in a manner with the utmost respect for the opponent. A player must not do things that will annoy or distract the opponent. It is important to maintain an honest and fair game.

The main goal of the game is to capture the opponent's King. But through the course of the game, it is necessary to capture other pieces in order to gain an advantage over the opposing side. A piece captures an opponent by moving and replacing the square it occupies. The piece is then removed from the chessboard after having been captured.

Chapter 2:

THE STARTING POSITION

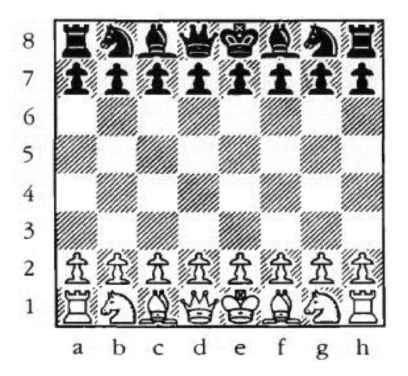

The diagram above shows how the different pieces are arranged on the chessboard at the beginning of every game. The pawns occupy the second rows from both ends of the board. So, from the white position, 8 pawns are in the second row or the 2nd rank.

While from the black side, another set of 8 pawns is in the second row, which is the 7th rank. The other pieces are arranged behind the pawns. This is why the pawn is often seen as the lowliest because they are often arranged to shield the important pieces like the Queen, king, etc., from direct attack.

After the pawns have taken their position, the two rooks are placed at the board's two extreme ends. After the rooks come to the knights and the bishops. While the king and Queen maintain the center position on the first row. The king usually starts on the e-file of the 1st rank while the Queen starts on the d-file of the same 1st rank.

One way to always remember and distinguish between the king and the Queen's starting positions is that the Queen always maintains the left-center position while the king maintains the right position. Alternatively, the Queen sits on the center square that has a light color. So, on a white row, the Queen will start on the light center square while the king rests on the remaining dark square.

How the Pieces Move

Chess is a board game played between two players. The chessboard is a square board made up of 64 alternating white and black squares (also called light and dark squares). At the beginning of the game, the chessboard is set up, as shown in the diagram below.

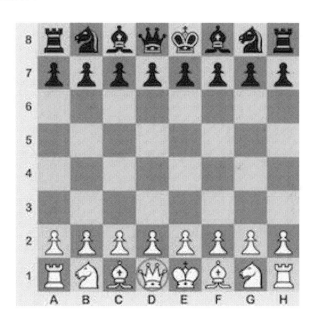

The color of the squares is important when setting up the chessboard. At the beginning of the game, the player with the white pieces is supposed to have a black square in their bottom left-hand corner and a white square in their bottom right-hand corner. This means that the white Queen (circled in the diagram above) is supposed to be on a white square. This also means that the black Queen is supposed to be on a black square.

The players make alternate moves, and the player with white pieces always moves first. Therefore, when the game begins, white will make a move, then black will make a move, then white, then black, then white, etc. Both players must always make a move when it is their turn; you aren't allowed to "pass" on your turn.

On each move you must move one of your pieces to a different square. Most of the pieces move in straight lines, so their moves are easy to remember, but there a few exceptions.

You win the game by "checkmating" your opponent. Simply put, checkmate means you have captured your opponent's king.

Let's now take a look at how each of the pieces moves.

The Pawn

Each player begins with 8 pawns, and they are generally (but not always) the weakest piece on the board. They are the weakest because their movement is generally the most limited of all the pieces. The pawn can move in one of 3 ways, depending on the situation (there is actually a special 4*th* way the pawn can move, but it's a bit complicated, so we'll come to it later):

1. You can move the pawn one square forwards to the square directly in front of it. The pawn can never move backward.

2. If a particular pawn has not been moved yet in the game, that pawn can move two squares forwards. Once you've moved that pawn, of course, you can only move that pawn one square forwards again each turn.

3. Pawns can only capture diagonally, one square to the upper-right or one square to the upper left.

The diagram below shows the 3 ways a pawn can move:

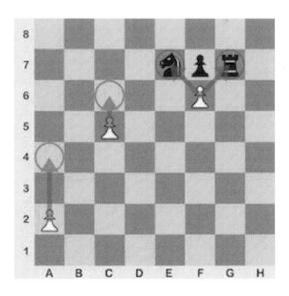

The first pawn on the left has not moved yet, so that you can move it 2 squares forwards to the circled square (you can also move it only 1 square forward if you want to). The second pawn to the right of it clearly has already moved, as it is not on its starting square, so if you want to move this pawn, you can only move it one square forward to the circled square. Finally, the third pawn, which is furthest on the right, can capture one of the enemy pieces diagonally in front of it. It can either capture the black knight who is one square to its upper-left, or it can capture the black rook, which is one square to its upper-right, but it cannot capture the enemy pawn, which is directly in front of it. In fact, the white pawn is blocked from moving forwards by the black pawn. If you wanted to move this white pawn, the only 2 moves you are allowed to make are to either to capture the black knight or to capture the black rook. Pawns can only capture pieces diagonally; they cannot capture pieces in front of them. This makes the pawn the only piece in the game that captures differently from it normally moves.

The pawn might seem boring so far, as it generally only plods directly forwards, but the pawn is actually the most special of all the pieces. This is because the pawn can transform into another piece. If you manage to plod your pawn forwards all the way to the end of the board, that pawn is said to be "Promoted," and you can transform that pawn into either a knight, bishop, rook, or Queen. Almost everyone chooses to transform their promoted pawns into a queen as the Queen is the best piece in the game. The diagrams below show this.

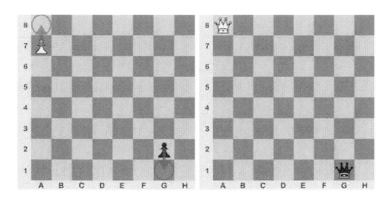

In the diagram on the left, both the white pawn on the left and the black pawn on the right is about to promote in one move. The white pawn will move one square forward and reach the end of the board and become a queen, and the black pawn will also move one square forward and become a queen. The diagram on the left shows what has happened on the next move—both the white and black pawns have been promoted and have become queens.

The Bishop

The bishop can move in a diagonal line as many squares as it likes. However, it cannot jump over other pieces (in fact, no piece can jump over another piece, except for the knight, which we will come to later). It can capture any enemy piece, which is on a square that it can move to. The diagram below shows the moves of a bishop:

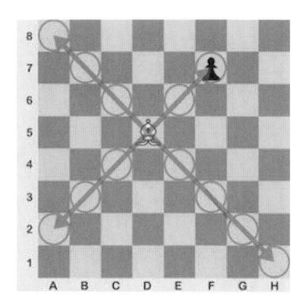

In the middle of the board in the diagram above, the white bishop can move to any of the circled squares. It can also capture the black pawn to its upper-right, but it cannot jump over it.

The Knight

The knight moves in an "L" shape. It moves two squares vertically and one to the side. Therefore, its range is quite short, unlike the bishop. The knight is the only piece that can jump over other pieces. It can jump over its own pieces and also enemy pieces. The knight can capture any enemy piece on a square that the knight can land on, but of course it cannot move to a square with one of its own pieces on it. The diagram below shows the moves of the knight.

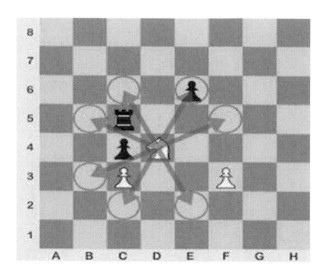

In the diagram above, the white knight has 7 possible moves. It can move to any of the 7 circled squares. The white knight can capture a black pawn, it can jump over the enemy rook or enemy pawn, and it can jump over its own pawn, but obviously, it cannot move to the square, which already has a white pawn on it.

The Rook

The rook's move is the simplest to understand of all the pieces. It moves in a straight line, either horizontally or vertically. It can move as many squares as it likes in a straight line. It can capture any enemy piece, which is in its way, but obviously cannot jump over other pieces. That's all there is to know about how the rook moves. The diagram below shows how the rook moves:

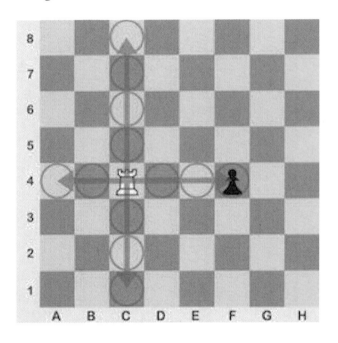

In the diagram above, the white rook has 12 possible moves. It can move to any of the 12-circled squares. It can capture the black pawn to its right, but it cannot jump over it.

The Queen

The Queen is the best piece in the game. It can move as many squares as it likes in a straight line horizontally, vertically, or diagonally. Therefore, it combines the moves of a rook and a bishop. It can capture any enemy piece in its way, but of course, it still cannot jump over other pieces. The diagram below shows the moves a queen can make:

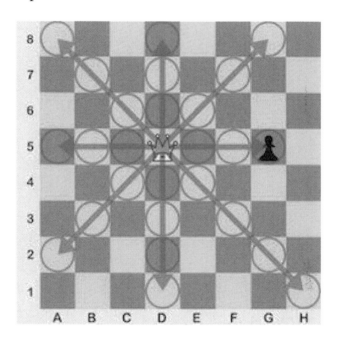

In the diagram above, the white Queen in the middle of the board has a whopping 26 available moves. It can move to any of the 26-circled squares, and it can capture the black pawn to the right of it. Obviously, pawns can also become queens when they reach the end of the board. Because the Queen is the best piece, most players try hard not to lose their Queen during the game.

The King

The Queen may be the most powerful piece on the board, but the king is the most important. If you lose your king, then you lose the game. The king can move one square in any direction. It can move up, down, left, right, or diagonally, but only one square at a time. Another way to say this is that the king can move to any square directly next to it. The king can also capture any piece, which is directly next to it. However, the king obviously cannot move to a square where an enemy piece can capture it. Well, I guess you could try to move your king to a square where it can be captured, but you would just automatically lose the game, so I wouldn't recommend it. The diagram below shows the moves of a king:

In the diagram above, the king has 6 available moves shown by the 6 circled squares. It can move to any of the squares next to it, except it can't move to the upper-left square because there it could be captured by a black's bishop, and it also can't move the square directly upwards from it as there it could be captured by black's pawn.

Capturing

You win the game by capturing your opponent's king, but to make it easier for you to do that, you generally try to remove as many of your opponents' pieces as possible. You do that by capturing your opponent's pieces. If an enemy piece is on a square that one of your pieces can move to, you can capture that enemy piece. You do this by removing the enemy piece from the board, and then your piece moves to the square where the enemy piece was. The exception to this is the pawn, which, as we've already mentioned, is the only piece that captures in a different way to how it moves. You cannot capture, or jump over, your own pieces. You cannot have two of your own pieces on the same square at the same time at any point during the game. I've already shown you a few examples of capturing when I was showing you the moves of the pieces, but to make it extra clear, I'll use another diagram below.

Step 1. It is white's move, and white is very happy because he can capture black's knight. White will move his rook to where the black knight is, and the black knight will be removed from the board:

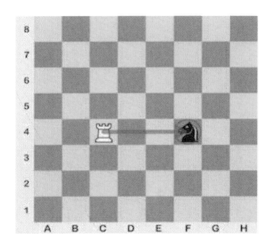

Step 2. This is the resulting position. Black's knight has been removed from the board, and white's rook is now where the black knight used to be:

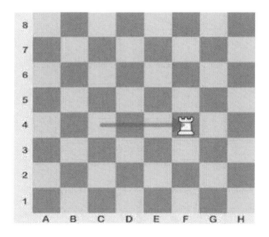

There are lots of different words that mean capture. Commonly chess players will say "captures," "takes," "eats," or even "kills." These words all mean the same thing—they are used when one piece captures or takes an enemy piece.

That's all the pieces' moves, but there are two more special moves in chess that I have to show you. They are called the "castling" move and the "en passant" move.

Special Moves

Aside from each piece's function in the game, there are special moves that each player can use to their advantage. These are as follows:

En Passant

It was mentioned earlier that pawns can capture opposing pieces diagonally. However, they can also capture other pawns through en passant (French words that mean "in passing"). This can happen if the opposing pawn moves two squares forward and that pawn lands beside your pawn.

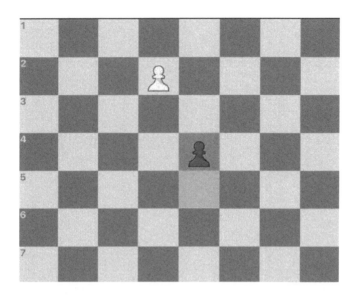

In the image above, Black just moved one square forward. Since white is still in its starting position, it can move 2 squares forward. It's also logical to take such a move, as it will avoid the usual way on how pawns capture other pieces.

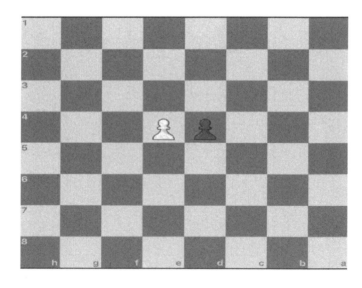

Let's suppose that White did move 2 squares forward, placing it beside Black's pawn.

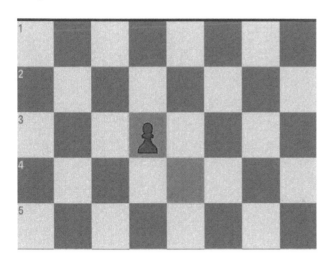

Though it seems like Black can't capture it, he still can do so with En Passant. Black simply has to move his pawn diagonally behind the pawn that moved 2 squares forward. The image above shows the movement made by Black, enabling him to capture White's pawn.

Pawn Promotion

If one will simply look at what the pawns can do, it's not surprising that those who are still learning the game consider them weak; after all, they have limited movement and a very short range for capturing opponents' pieces. However, once a pawn reaches the last rank on the enemy's side of the board, it can be promoted and become a piece with a higher value.

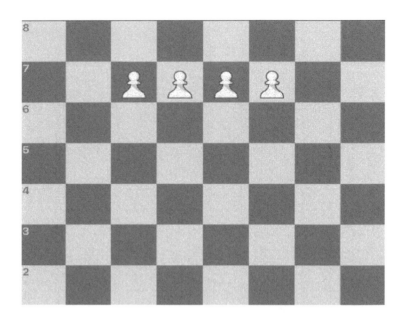

The image above shows 4 white pawns that are ready for promotion. These pawns can become any other piece aside from the King. Most players promote their pawns to become a Queen, as it has the most range. It's even possible to have multiple Queens! The piece can also be promoted to a piece that is lower than the Queen (called underpromotion), as the choice entirely depends on what the players want and needs.

Castling

This move can only be done once in a game, and it needs the rooks and the King to be in their starting positions (and have never been moved) before it can be used.

To do this, simply move the king two squares towards the rook, then move the rook as if it jumped over the king and landing next to it.

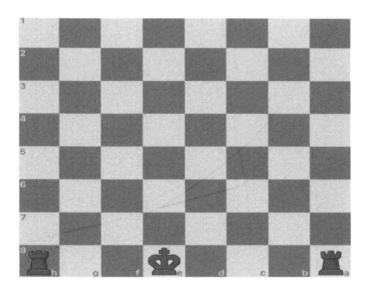

The image above shows the positions of the pieces before castling. This move cannot be made if pieces are obstructing the path of the king and rook. Castling to the left is called king-side castling (or castling short), while castling on the left is called queen-side castling (or castling long).

Aside from the path to castling being unobstructed and the pieces are not yet moved, 3 special rules should also be remembered before one can castle:

- One cannot castle if they are in check.

- Castling can't be done if the king will be moving to a square that will put it in check.

- This move cannot be made if the destination square of the king will put it in check.

In the image above, it can be seen that White's King is in check, violating Rule 1. In order for him not to lose his ability to castle, he should get out of check by moving the bishop in front of it.

The image above shows how rules 2 and 3 are being violated. The Queen's movement to a green square puts one square on the path to castling under threat for the king. Rule 3 is observed if one will look at the diagonal path of the Queen. Since the king's landing square will result in a check. For this situation, one can simply capture the Queen by using the White Pawn.

In this image, although it violates rule 2 for castling long, he can still castle short because its squares are not under threat for the king.

Chapter 3:

CHESS NOTATION

Chess notation is the common name for writing down all the moves of a chess game. This is required for tournament play because a record of the moves is required in case of a dispute by one or both players.

It's also a good idea to get in the habit of recording your moves, even if you're just playing for fun. That will allow you to analyze your games to see where you made mistakes so you can correct them.

The official chess rulebook states that you can take notes virtually any way you want, as long as anyone else can understand and interpret the game. There have been many chess notation methods developed over the years, the most common of which is algebraic notation. So, let's learn that one:

First, you need to have a chessboard with the algebraic coordinates on it. This is the same board mentioned at the beginning of the book. As noted earlier, the squares are labeled vertically from bottom to top with the numbers 1 through 8 on the white player's side and horizontally from left to right with the letters a through h.

The pieces must also be labeled. We use the letter *K* for the king, the letter *Q* for the Queen, the letter *B* for the bishop, the letter *N* for the knight (because the letter K is already used for the king), and the letter *R* for the rook. These single-letter designations are capitalized when written. Pawns are not indicated by a letter but by their movement, as you will see.

We then use a combination of the piece name and the appropriate square on the board to record a move. For instance, if you moved a bishop to the e5 square, you would write *Be5*. If you moved the Queen to the g6 square, you would write *Qg6*.

It's even simpler to write a pawn move. For example, to move a pawn from e2 to e4, you would simply write "e4," which is the square where the pawn ends up.

The letter *x* is used when capturing the opponent's material. For instance, if one of your opponent's pieces is on h4, and you capture it with your knight, you would write "Nxh4." If you capture your opponent's piece on h4 with your pawn that was on the "g" file, you will simply write "gxh4."

Sometimes you'll want to move a piece and notice that another piece can also move to the same square. As an example, suppose you have a knight on b1 and another knight on f3. You want to move the b1 knight to d2, but you notice that the f3 knight can also move to d2, as shown in Exhibit 14.

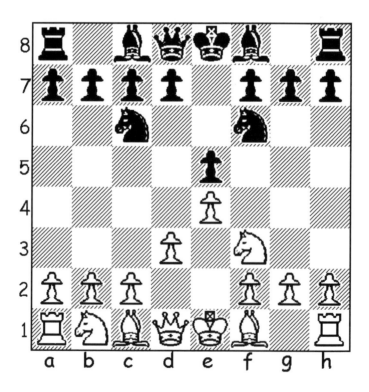

If you simply write "Nd2," how would you know which knight you moved to the d2 square when you review this game in the future? The answer is to write "Nbd2." The letter "b" written prior to the move, which in this case is d2, indicates which knight was moved.

Pawns reaching the final rank and achieving promotion into the piece of your choice—to note this, a pawn reaching g8 and promoting to a queen would be written, "g8 Q" for the Queen. You may also see it written as "g8=Q."

Castling, in which the king and rook are moved in one move, is written as follows: when castling to the kingside, you would write O-O. When the king is castled to the queenside, which is a longer move than kingside castling, the slightly longer notation of O-O-O would be used.

If you put someone in check, the plus sign (+) is normally used. Checkmate is normally denoted with the number sign (#). When the game is over, you show a game won by white as 1-zero, a game won by black as zero-1, and a draw as ½-½.

Chapter 4:

BASIC OPENING STRATEGIES

The opening ranks begin to mobilize as the pawns start their slow march across the board. Knights take to the field, aiming to thin enemy formations, while bishops begin seeking out the slightest chink in the opposing defense, ready to lash out and escalate the game into an all-out war. The opening game is where strategists begin laying out their elaborate plans, carefully preparing to spring them into action when the time arises.

In technical terms, the opening game is defined as the first few moves of play, where pieces are developed and formations assembled. If that doesn't sound overly specific, it's because it's not. There are no absolute delineations between a chess game's phases, and often openings and middlegames will overlap.

Chess openings have been studied perhaps more than any other facet of the game, in no small part because many top-level games are won and lost in just the first few moves. Many critical exchanges can take place even in just the first few moves. Even if you're not directly capturing an opponent's piece, shutting down their best-laid plans can establish a dominating positional and mental advantage.

Like any stage of the game, there are boundless ways your opening strategy can take shape. While extreme high-level players study and memorize openings up to dozens of moves, there's no need to be intimidated. While opening strategy is an important aspect of play at any level, it's only one of several stages that make up the full chess strategy scope.

There are millions of ways a chess game can evolve based on just the first few moves. Still, the most strategically sound openings have been divided into three basic categories: Flank Openings, King's Pawn Openings, and Queen's Pawn Openings. Each of these three categories branches out into dozens of divisions and subdivisions. Still, we'll review just a few of the most popular variations and explore what makes them so effective.

King's Pawn Openings

From turn one, White has 20 possible opening moves, and the King's Pawn Opening of e4 is widely considered as one of the most popular and efficient. This may take new players somewhat by surprise, as it seems to leave the king's file exposed to attack. However, mounting a practical attack on the king remains largely infeasible, especially if White takes advantage of the opportunity to develop both their Queen and bishop.

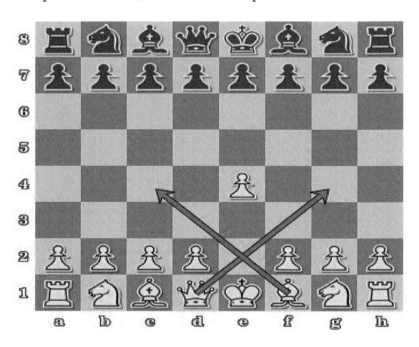

The King's Pawn Opening begins with White's pawn moving to e4. From there, two more powerful pieces can quickly be deployed.

In addition to speeding the development of the Queen, e4 is a strong opening because it establishes an early presence at the board's center. While the downside of this is that White's pawn is temporarily undefended, the player has an opportunity to quickly reinforce it with a robust formation of pawns and harder-hitting pieces.

After such a strong opening, how is Black meant to answer? The most common answer to the King's Pawn Opening is the Sicilian Defense of c5. In fact, this is one of the most common opening exchanges in all of chess. The stark difference in the strategy behind White and Black's opening moves in this scenario perfectly highlights the distinctions of playing as either of the two sides.

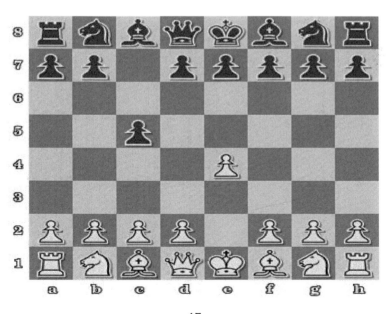

In the Sicilian Defense, unlike White, Black's first move to c5 does little to develop pieces. However, there are other substantial advantages.

Whereas White almost always holds an early lead by holding a default initiative, Black must struggle to both halt White's advantage and seize one of their own. Thus, while White's first move in the King's Pawn Opening focuses on asserting quick dominance and pushing a plan into action, the Sicilian Defense is a more reserved response. Black offers White the opportunity to take control of the kingside files quickly, but in exchange, a powerful phalanx of Black's pawns can dominate the queenside field. If Black acts quickly, they can establish their own zone of control while creating a thorny shield against White's attack.

Alternatively, Black may opt for the even more conservative Caro-Kann Defense, in which the pawn moves only one space to c6. This is generally a move favored by more strategic players who seek to establish a long-term positional advantage and are less concerned with opening exchanges.

Of course, some players prefer direct and immediate confrontation. If dynamic play is more of your style, you might answer the King's Pawn Opening with e5 or an Open Game. White will often answer with Nf3, threatening Black's pawn, to which the most common response is Nc6. From there, White attacks the developed knight with Bb5, creating the Ruy Lopez or Spanish Game.

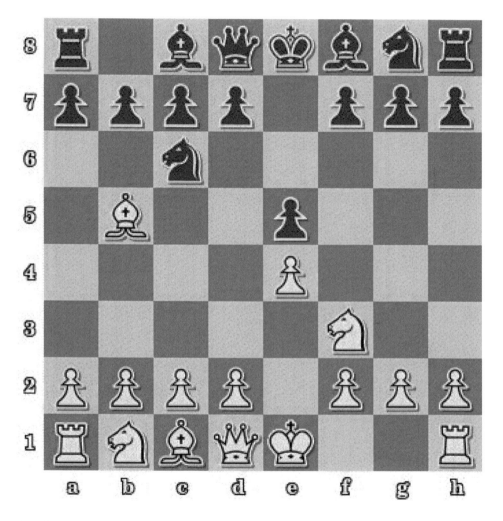

In the Ruy Lopez opening pictured above, threats are made quickly, and both players must leap to action.

One of the fantastic things about the Ruy Lopez is that it offers several viable moves for both sides at almost every point throughout the game. Ruy Lopez offers quick-thinking tacticians a veritable buffet line of attacks and gambits to pursue in contrast to more formulaic approaches. In fact, there are so many different chains of play that can arise from this opening that it has become one of the most studied phenomena in chess.

While King's Pawn Openings are the most common in high-level play, they're far from the only viable opening strategies. While opening the pawn on the Queen's file may not be as popular, it does provide some distinct advantages.

Queen's Pawn Openings

Like the King's Pawn Opening, this opening emphasizes controlling the board's center from the outset. To begin the game by moving to d4, White prepares to develop the queenside bishop and potentially perform the more difficult queenside castling.

A classic evolution of this opening occurs when black responds with d5, and White proceeds to offer the Queen's Gambit by moving another pawn to c4. Here, Black is faced with a hard decision. They may choose to accept the offered pawn with dxc4, but doing so gives White total control of the center. Alternatively, in denying the bait, Black allows White to pen them in.

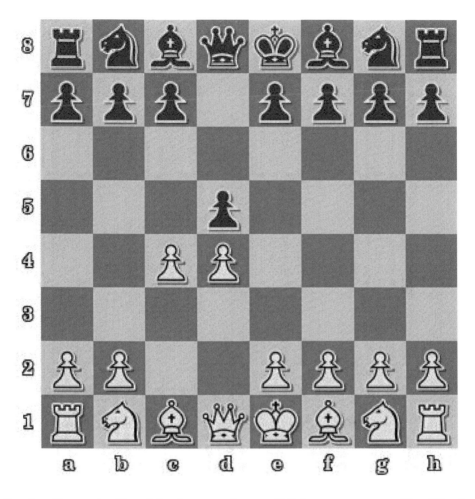

In the Queen's Gambit shown above, White seems to offer Black a pawn, but the gift is poisoned with a difficult choice.

While the Queen's Gambit was extremely popular in the early 20th century, developments in the hypermodern school led to an increasing number of players adopting the Indian Defense and its variations. With this strategy, Black instead opts for the somewhat unusual first-round play of Nf6. Rather than confront White's opening or even attempting to establish their own center of power, Black begins to develop an elaborate web meant to undermine White's supposedly free development.

There are several possible progressions of the Indian Defense, but one of the strongest and most commonly seen in all play levels is the Nimzo-Indian Defense. In this variation, Black opts to remain flexible for several turns, delaying the building of their own pawn structure with the sole intent of hindering White's.

The standard Nimzo-Indian Defense evolves as such:

- d4 Nf6

- c4 e6

- Nc3 Bb4

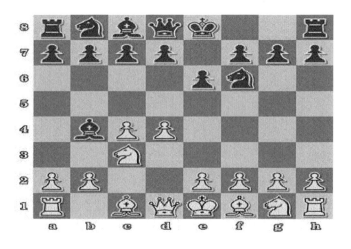

In the Nimzo-Indian Defense, Black opts to quickly field their kingside bishop, knowing it will most likely be sacrificed in due time.

While both the King and Queen's Pawn Openings derive much of their power from establishing a strong presence in the center, there are always other viable options. The final main category of opening, called the Flank openings, seek to exploit the very concept of central control.

Flank Openings

A reference to military flanking maneuvers, in which one force intercepts the other from the side rather than head-on, the Flank openings avoid the center of the board and threaten from the sides. While any number of different opening moves could be considered a Flank opening, the two most common are 1. Nf3, and 1. c4.

The simplest of the two, 1. c4, is often referred to as the English Opening. In addition to the obvious opportunity to field the Queen, this opening also gives White several viable strategies to fall back on, making it difficult for Black to counter. For example, White can easily shift back into a Queen's Gambit or advance into the Réti Opening to threaten from both flanks.

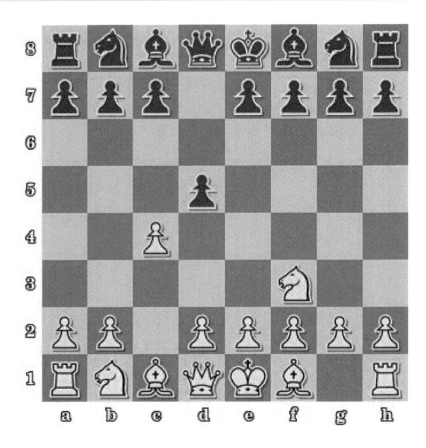

In stark contrast to the King or Queen's pawn openings, the Réti Opening controls the center from outside rather than within.

The Réti Opening is itself normally played as a progression of the Zukertort Opening—the name given to 1. Nf3. Much like the Indian Defenses, which also emphasize the quick deployment of knights, this opening is a strong example of the Hypermodern School of strategy. In contrast to the classical school, which tends to engage in tactical play, hypermodern players tend to be more fluid strategists. The Réti Opening exemplifies their belief that while the board's center is an important strategic asset, it is controlled most effectively by outside threats rather than a direct confrontation.

Choosing Your Opening

You've familiarized yourself with the four most popular opening moves: 1. e4, 1. d4, 1. c4, and 1. Nf3. You've also learned ways to advance the game from these openings, whether you're playing on Black or White's side. While various masters have theorized on which of these strategies is the strongest, the truth is that no single sequence of moves will allow you to win every game or even most games. If that were the case, chess would almost certainly lose most of its appeal as a pastime!

Rather than searching for an answer on what the "strongest" opening is, ask yourself instead, what openings are most suited to your style of play? Do you prefer straightforward play rooted firmly in tactical prowess? The King's Pawn Openings may serve you well, while the Queen's Pawn Openings and the Queen's Gambit may be of use to those who enjoy a balance of flexibility in direct confrontation. Or, if you're mostly interested in outmaneuvering and out scheming your opponents, then the Flank openings may be your most enjoyable path to victory.

You'll also need to consider your opponent if you have enough information to do so. If your opponent has you outmatched in raw tactics, consider a slower-paced opening that will allow you to build out a secured strategy before engaging. On the other hand, you might counter a brilliant strategist with an explosive and direct offensive play that prevents them from setting up their elaborate plans. Above all, always try to keep your opponent guessing and on their toes.

The early exchanges of the opening can produce ripples that are felt throughout the game. However, don't assume that losing your first battle means you've lost the war. Likewise, never assume that your opening strategy was so effective that you could begin to let your guard down. A game of chess can turn over on its head with just a few moves.

Unlike the openings and endgames, the middlegame seems to be the least heavily studied chess strategy area. However, if one thing is true in chess, it's that no detail can ever be overlooked. As you read on, keep these opening strategies in mind, and consider how they can inform your play as we move into the next major play phase.

Chapter 5:

BASIC MIDDLE
GAME STRATEGIES

The opening of chess games though not entirely easy is simpler to comprehend compared to the middlegame. The middle game is challenging to very many players. As a beginner player, you get to the middlegame where both players have developed their pieces, and it's time to kick things off seriously and become overwhelming.

The middlegame can simply be said to be the race to dominance. This is where most objectives are attained. Maintaining a lead in the middlegame is key in ensuring victory in the endgame. The possible plays in the endgame are unlimited, almost infinite. This is the part of the game where very many things can go differently.

A well-played middlegame can lead to a very lengthy game. Also, it's possible to make a serious mistake and turn the middlegame into an instant endgame.

Areas of Focus In the Middlegame

1. Maintaining Lead

You are still in the race to achieving all the set 5 objectives, and the middlegame is basically where the race takes form. This stage is usually all about the objectives more than anything else. If you had a lead in the opening, make sure you maintain it by keeping your opponent on the defensive. Careful not to make any mistake at this point as it can be quite costly.

2. Space Advantage

Now that a number of pieces have been captured and others developed the room in the board to fight for seems to have increased. The goal is to ensure you control the center as this guarantees you control most parts of the board and having several local area majorities. Space on the board gives your pieces room to breathe and move around easily. This poses more danger to your opponent. Achieve this by blockades against the enemy and capturing to advantage.

3. Improving Pawn Structure

Pawn structure starts to take form in the middlegame. Look at your pawn structure and evaluate what can be done to improve it. Be careful not to end up with pawn-islands. Fix any if already exist. Try and establish a queenside majority to help in the endgame.

4. Piece Mobility

Having just one-piece mobility over the enemy is of great advantage. Try and make your pieces as mobile as possible. Don't have blocked pieces or underutilized ones.

5. Rook Freedom

Rook is a very important force in a chess game and can wreak serious havoc. Your goal is to ensure that he has freedom. A strategically placed rook on one end of a file or rank poses a great risk to a larger area on the board and cuts off most pieces from each other's support. Try to have your rooks on open files or ranks where they can do the most damage.

6. Pairing Forces

This applies to the bishop and rooks. Two rooks occupying open rank or files cover a bigger part of the board but are not as safe compared to pairing them together on a single rank or file. The same applies to the bishop. Take a long diagonal and pair your bishops to offer a stronger attacking force.

7. Major Control

Again, for bishops and rooks. A full rank and file controlled by a rook reduce the space for the opponent on the board, and we both know how important space is. If you can control the long diagonals and an additional rank or file, you can have a space advantage over the enemy, which you can translate into a material advantage.

8. Weak Squares

Try and create as many weak squares as you can in enemy territory and occupy them. This is the part where you penetrate into enemy territory and start threatening their king to create tempo. The earlier you can gain tempo over the enemy, the earlier you can solidify your lead.

9. Exchange

Gain a material advantage by exchanging his valuable pieces. Try to have more points on the board than the enemy as you get to the endgame. Be careful not to lose important endgame pieces in the exchange. Your preference for endgames determines this. Keep the pieces that you are good at ending the game with.

10. King Safety

King safety part of the objective manifests itself in the middlegame as well as other objectives. If you hadn't castled in the opening, you should definitely do it and cover your king. Threaten the enemy's king safety to create tempo. Though unlikely, mount attacks on the king to force the enemy into a careless move that drives them to an earlier losing endgame.

Chapter 6:

BASIC ENDGAME STRATEGIES

The smoke clears across the field of battle, and only a scarce few combatants remain standing on either side. Either both players have executed their middlegame strategies and oppose one another with their favored pieces at the ready, or one player has taken a decisive advantage. It may be a long, brutal hunt before the enemy king is cornered, or it might happen in a single fatal instant. In either case, the endgame is upon them, and only one can win.

As we've already established, phases of play are somewhat malleable, and there's not necessarily a clear indicator of when the endgame begins. In fact, it's not unusual for a king to be checkmated in the middlegame and for the game to close with no endgame at all.

However, a game of chess can be said to have entered its endgame when both players have been reduced to only a few pieces and their kings. Remember, pawns are not considered "pieces" in the technical terms of the game. Often, a pawn's advantage can be the deciding factor in who emerges from the endgame victorious.

In most endgame scenarios, the player who gained a material advantage in the endgame should generally seek to make as many aggressive material trades as possible without sacrificing any pawn. That player's remaining piece(s) can protect pawns on their way to promotion, which is often a death knell for the enemy king. Of course, endgames are extremely varied, and not all of them end with a promoted pawn.

Finally, endgames are characterized by the play's shift where the king becomes a much more powerful offensive tool. Crafty players can weaponize their king to wipe out an opponent's pawn formations or even back the opposing king into a tough spot.

Much like openings, chess endgames are a topic that has been studied extensively throughout the game's history. You can buy dozens of books dedicated to exploring the various endgame scenarios (often called "positions"), many of which feature theoretical exercises that allow students of the game to test their wit and skill. In this guide, we'll focus mainly on the various types of endgames and what beginners need to know to achieve checkmate in each of them.

Endgames Without Pawns

Because of the importance of pawns in the endgame, many players will attempt to eliminate the threat of enemy promotion by wiping their opponent's pawns out entirely. This results in some endgames where there are no remaining pawns at all.

In these scenarios, a king and either a queen or a rook can easily achieve a checkmate against an opponent. Paired bishops on opposite colors also have a fairly simple time achieving checkmate. A bishop and knight will have a much more difficult time, and with two knights, it is nearly impossible to checkmate an opponent, especially if they have a few pieces remaining on the board.

The primary threat in an endgame with no remaining pawns is the possibility of an opponent forcing a draw through a stalemate. Ironically, this becomes somewhat easier for a king pitted against a king and Queen, especially if the player with more material is less experienced. Due to the Queen's vast range of threatened squares, a wily player can slip their king into position for a stalemate.

Assuming it's Black's move, this game ends in a stalemate. This is undoubtedly a frustrating prospect for the dominant player.

Fortunately, this type of stalemate is usually easy to avoid once you've become aware of it. Simply remain aware of where your opponent can move on their next turn and ensure there's always at least one safe square available.

Another major factor in endgames with very few pieces, like those discussed here, is the concept of opposition. Opposition occurs when two kings are separated from each other only by one rank or file. In this scenario, the player whose turn it is to move has no choice, but to move their king away from the enemy, assuming the king is the only piece they can move.

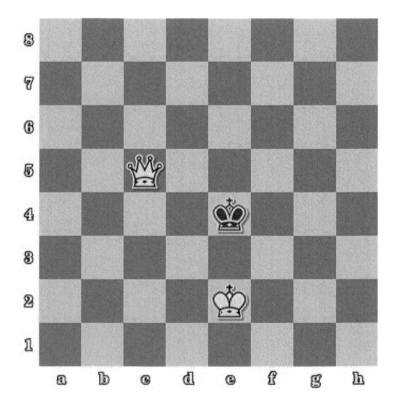

Assuming Black's turn to move, White's king uses opposition to effectively threaten the three squares directly in front of it, cutting off almost half of Black's options for movement and forcing them into an increasingly difficult position.

Opposition can be a decisive factor in nearly every endgame scenario, but it plays an especially critical role in endgames without pawns and — ironically — endgames with only pawns.

King and Pawn Endgames

Sometimes an endgame results in all pieces being captured on both sides, leaving only the kings and their remaining pawns. More than any other endgame, having more pawns than your opponent is key to victory in these scenarios, especially if you have passed pawns on their way to promotion.

In any case, precision is key in a king and pawn endgame, and this becomes truer with the fewer pawns that are remaining on the board. The classic king and pawn vs king endgame have been analyzed endlessly by strategists for this very reason. A single error can turn a win into a draw or a draw into a loss in such a contest.

In a king and pawn vs king endgame, each player's objective becomes clear: the player with the pawn must promote it to achieve checkmate, while the lone king must prevent that outcome in order to secure a draw. To do so, the lone king must either capture the enemy pawn or occupy the square directly in front of that pawn or the square in front of that. By doing so, the lone king can simply cycle through positions to keep the game going indefinitely without the pawn progressing, thereby forcing a draw.

So long as Black plays without error, this game could continue forever. Black has succeeded in forcing a draw.

In these scenarios, where success or failure rides on every single movement, the concept of triangulation is essential for both parties. Basically, triangulation in chess refers to the ability of a piece (almost always the king) to return to the same position in three moves. Usually, triangulation also refers to the tactic in which this maneuvering is used to gain a positional advantage over the opponent.

Triangulation can be a tricky concept to grasp in the abstract. To better understand it, let's refer back to the diagram above, but with a few added visual aids.

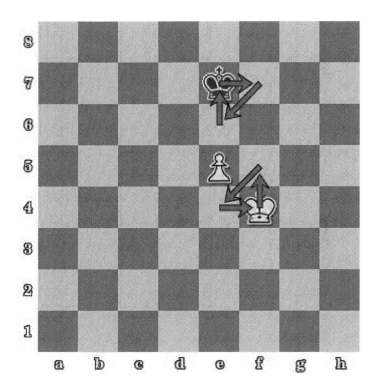

The reason Black can successfully force a draw is because of triangulation.

In this scenario, Black's king must prevent the pawn from progressing, and White's king must remain within one square of the pawn to protect it as it advances. As long as Black continuously cycles through Ke7, Kf7, and Ke6—and always counters White's Kf5 with Kf7—Black will succeed at forcing a draw through the use of triangulation and opposition.

However, if Black isn't properly triangulating, White can also use the same concepts to win. If White can reach a position on Kf5 and Black makes the mistake of responding with Ke7, White will have gained a fatal upper hand. White's pawn can finally advance to e6 while still being protected by its king, and Black will have no choice but to retreat. This is the only scenario in which a long king can still lose when controlling the two squares directly in front of the final pawn in this type of endgame.

In this scenario, Black would likely have preferred not to make a move at all, and simply hold their blocking position indefinitely. However, the rules of chess mandate that each player must move one piece each round. The idea that a player might be forced to move even when it's against their best interests is called zugzwang. It's a concept that permeates chess and many other turn-based games, but it's particularly important in chess endgames.

Like that of opposition, triangulation and zugzwang are both key concepts to be aware of in any endgame strategy. Not only are they individually important tactical tools, when used together, they also turn your king into an offensive powerhouse capable of turning the tide as the game draws to a close. Now that you've been introduced to all three, you're ready to study some of the other possible endgame scenarios. As you read on, try to think about strategic roles your king could play in each possible endgame.

King and Knight Endgames

The knight is the most difficult piece to deliver checkmate with, since its features are relatively few during endgames, as many players choose to exchange theirs during the middlegame. While a knight can't deliver checkmate on its own, it can work well in tandem with other pieces. Since you can never be sure when you might be forced to enter the endgame leaning heavily on a remaining knight, it's best to understand their endgame strategy, even if it isn't optimal.

Against pawns, a knight's primary objective is to use its jumping ability to weave through enemy blockades and pick off pawns one at a time. A passed pawn can be a nuisance, but the knight should be able to block it, if not capture it before it can promote.

Unfortunately, relying on a knight to stand against rooks, queens, or even bishops often means you're aiming to draw rather than win. The good news is, knights are much more capable defenders in the endgame than they are attackers. By keeping your knight and king close to one another, both pieces can work in tandem to support one another, making it easy enough to draw against stronger piece like a rook.

Figure 30: this is a difficult endgame for Black, but not impossible.

In the figure above, Black must stop the advance of the enemy pawn if they're to force a draw. Black's knight will have difficulty capturing the passed pawn, but it can easily block and provide defensive cover while the Black king moves to capture. If the player can pull this off, Black will successfully draw by keeping the king and knight close together and able to protect one another.

With just a few more pieces in play, the knight's defensive capabilities become more of an asset. Even two knights can protect each other and the king well enough to force a draw, if not significantly outnumbered. Still, the knight is generally not a preferred piece to be brought into the endgame and should be sacrificed in favor of a more powerful offensive weapon if possible.

King and Bishop Endgames

While certainly a more versatile attacker in the endgame than a knight, a lone bishop remains incapable of forcing a checkmate. This becomes significantly more manageable with a pair of bishops since they're both on opposite-colored squares.

One notorious endgame scenario is when each player has only a bishop and pawns remaining, but the bishops are on opposite colors. Since the bishops cannot attack each other, they must be used primarily as defensive tools to support the players' remaining pawns. This is one of the few cases where a "bad" bishop penned in by surrounding pawns is actually an advantage, as it can provide superior protection.

Bishops are also known for being involved in one of the most common pawnless endgames: a rook and bishop versus one rook. In this scenario, the player with the material generally wins by using the bishop to chase the defender's rook away from squares that allow it to protect its king. With this done, the attacker's rook and king can corner the enemy and achieve a checkmate.

A common counter to this that allows the materially weaker player to draw is the Cochrane Defense. Named after the chess master John Cochrane, the defending player uses the rook to effectively pin the bishop to its king near the board's center. With only the enemy's rook left as a credible threat, the defender can often force a draw.

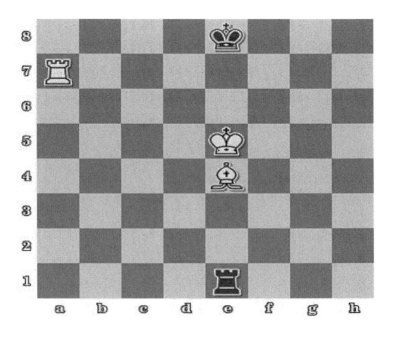

From this position (the Cochrane Defense); Black can endlessly stall out the game with a bit of clever play.

Ultimately, unless they're paired together, bishops are supporters in the endgame, not attackers. As we move on to the more aggressive role of the major pieces in the final game, keep in mind how knights and bishops can be used to support these more powerful pieces if you find yourself with any of these remaining pieces as the game draws to a close.

King and Rook Endgames

Rook endgames are among the most common and best-studied endgames. This is partly because they are always being late to develop and are quite valuable; rooks are not generally exchanged until very late in the game. Another factor is that rook endgames can be extremely complex. On an open board, a rook can generally lock out any rank or file combination in a matter of two moves, often less. This makes pawn promotion much more difficult than in endgames featuring mostly minor pieces.

Especially in a rook and pawn endgame, positioning your rook on the seventh rank can spell doom for your opponent. There are no guarantees, but a rook that controls the seventh rank can sweep up undeveloped pawns while protecting its advancing allies. A famous example comes from the 1924 contest between

Jose Raul Capablanca and Savielly Tartakower. In this match, Capablanca successfully infiltrated the enemy lines with his rook leading into the endgame. After a fairly even contest, Tartakower was defenseless against this sudden threat.

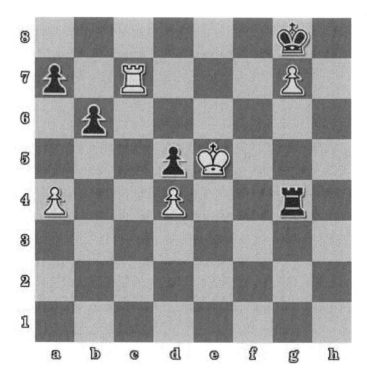

Materially, this endgame may seem dead even, but White's Rook is far better positioned to provide an overwhelming advantage.

Take the diagram above as an example. Assuming Black is to move, they're faced with two equally disastrous options, all thanks to White's rook. They could continue holding back White's pawn with the king, but White's rook will continue to wreak havoc on their pawns. Black could capture the pawn on g7 with their rook, which almost certainly ends with a rook exchange. While Black would end that exchange with one additional pawn, White's king is still far better positioned to support its fewer pawns on their way to promotion. Black almost certainly loses this match.

This is the general principle behind rook endgames — aggression. The rook must seek to wipe out as much enemy material as possible, both to gain a material advantage and increase its mobility.

King and Queen Endgames

Despite its tremendous power, the Queen appears in a significantly lower number of endgames than the rook. This may be because queens tend to be more active in the middlegame than the rooks, generally having the side-effect of them being exchanged or otherwise captured before the endgame can begin. Another reason is that due to the Queen's ability to overwhelm the enemy while active on the board, many games where the Queen is not captured come to an end before a proper endgame can be declared.

If you do hold onto your Queen into the endgame, it's a powerful asset. Even on its own, the Queen can easily work in tandem with your king to force a checkmate. As with a rook, however, the goal of your Queen coming into the endgame should be to eliminate any pesky pawn—especially passed pawns—that your opponent still controls. A queen's limitations are perhaps the best illustration of how important the king and pawns become in the endgame.

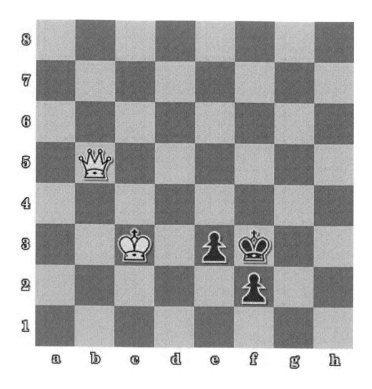

Despite the massive material imbalance, Black still has many paths leading to victory since it already has two passed pawns close to being promoted.

In the figure above, Black has created a strong fortress—a formation of pieces that both defend the king and allow the king to defend them. White would have a bout of difficult play ahead even if Black's pawns were still further back, but their position on the second and third ranks makes this situation truly dire. As long as Black keeps a strong formation, White cannot capture without losing their Queen, and may as well lose the game. Due to White's poor positioning, Black is likely to be victorious here.

Part of the problem is that the White King and Queen are not positioned to support each other in this example. White's best option is for the king to move to d4 and attempt to capture on e3, but by then, Black will have a promoted pawn defended by its king, and the match becomes materially even.

A far better example of the King and Queen working in tandem comes from the 18th-century player François-André Danican Philidor. With both an opening and endgame position named for him, Philidor's chess analysis contributions are quite weighty.

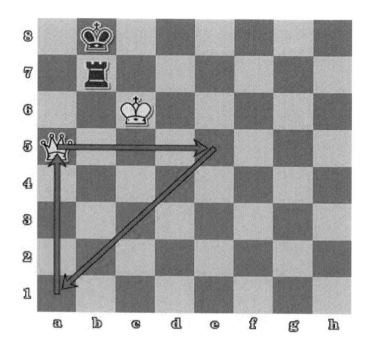

Here, White's King and Queen are working in perfect sync, forcing black into zugzwang if needed, and securing a victory.

In this position, analyzed by Philidor, Black is experiencing zugzwang if they're to move, their rook forced to abandon its king and weaken both of their positions. If White is to move, they can easily force Black into the same state of zugzwang by triangulating with the Queen, keeping Black's king in constant check during the process.

Make no mistake—the Queen is a fantastic asset in any endgame. However, if there's one thing to learn from this section, it's that positional advantages make more of a difference in the endgame than in any other phase. A poorly positioned queen is easily thwarted by two well-placed pawns, after all.

But what about the human element? We've weighed material factors and positional factors, but if that were all there was to it, chess would be a rather boring game. The truth is, no scenario ever has a truly predestined outcome.

Endgame Theory vs Reality

Some of the earliest documentation we have on chess analysis has to do with endgame studies. It's a topic that's been analyzed back and forth endlessly over generations of expert players. Today, computer analysis has brought this field of study to new heights, with online databases called tablebases enabling theorists to review exhaustive analysis of endgame positions.

With so much scholarship on the subject, many guides you might refer to will show you a position on the board and state simply that White is sure to win in a certain number of moves. The critical element to remember here is that such declarations assume perfect play on both sides. Two queens can certainly outmaneuver a queen in the endgame, but few actual players are also likely to possess the skill to do so too.

Assuming you're playing against others of your skill level, don't be discouraged by high-level theory. These complex scenarios are often meant to illustrate unusual and extreme cases and shouldn't be something you expect to encounter. While master-level players might attempt to reverse-engineer these specific scenarios, for us, they're theoretical illustrations of key concepts that can have a more practical effect on endgame strategy.

By combining your knowledge of key endgame tactics — opposition, triangulation, fortresses, and zugzwang, you'll stand a much better chance in an endgame scenario. On top of that, you're now equipped to circle back and apply what you know about all three phases of the game to each other. From setting up in the opening to exchanging in the middlegame, you now possess the tools needed to formulate your own comprehensive chess strategies.

Of course, just like endgame analysis, a study can only ever take you so far. Now that you have the tools, it's time to start putting them into action.

Chapter 7:

CHECKMATING PATTERNS

In a chess recreation, you ought to take a look at the opposite king. It will help you practice the elements because of the loading agent.

Thanks to this guide, you may enhance your vision at the chessboard, and you may discover spouses faster.

Anastasia's spouse is a general manner to test. The officer took his name from the radical Anastasia und das Schachspiel by means of Johann Jakob Wilhelm Heinz. It is executed the usage of a knight and a crusher to trap and take a look at the black king.

Andersen's Colleague

Andersen's wife is a well-known manner to test and is known as Adolf Anderson. This officer uses a white rook or a queen to check the black king.

The boot is supported using a pedestrian or a bishop. Anderson's wife is frequently visible before, and very little can be finished to save her.

Arab Neighbor

The wife of Saudi Arabia is a general way to test. The verification officer works with the knight so that the king's diagonal squares are black, so he can capture him with a rook to prepare the check. This dealer can test the rank or report.

The Player Behind the Rank

The back pair is a fashionable manner to test. It takes place that a collar or Queen controls a king who is blocked through his thick (mainly pedestrian) pieces inside the first or eighth row, and there is virtually no manner to carry the attacking piece to the troubled king. For example, the Black Queen cannot capture the white rook.

Bishop and Knight of the Maidana

The bishop and knight officer is a well-known way to check. It takes place that the king and his thick pieces pressure the bishop and knight, the king of the adversary, at the nook of the photo that the bishop can manipulate so that he can deliver his spouse. It is also possible to use urgent the missing king in the deadlock, in which he can be checked.

However, of the four critical missions, along with Queen Kate, Box Matt, and King, and the 2 suspicious purposes of the bishops, that is a part of the husband's hardest strengths, as he can play 34 full-sport games. Sometimes the result is a draw.

Blackburn's Wife

Blackburn's spouse is known as Joseph Henry Blackburn and is an unusual way to check. Using a black liquor (in place of a bishop or Queen), the Czech officer restricts the black king's getaway in square f8. One of the bishops restricts the black king's motion by using lengthy operating distances, while the knight and bishop work nearby. Blackburn's spouse's threats may be used to weaken Black's function.

Matt Field

Matt Box is a part of the 4 most important missions with the Queen's spouse, the king, and the 2 bishops of the bishops and bishops and knights. It occurs like the king's side and the king's pavement container empty to the corner or the plank's aspect.

Corner Couple

A corner couple is a popular manner to test. It is executed by locking the king in a nook using a rook and a queen and using a knight to lease the managing officer.

Cosio's Wife

Cosio's spouse is a fashionable manner to test. The checkmate is an inverted model of Dovetail's husband. It became named after an observation conducted in 1766 by Carlo Cosio.

Similar to Bishop Damiano

Bishop Damiano is an incredible direction to verify. The verification officer makes use of the Queen and the bishop, wherein the bishop is used to support the Queen, and the Queen is conversant in engaging inside the mission. The checkmate is named after Pedro Damiano.

Damiano's Colleague

Damiano's wife is an excellent way to check one of the oldest. It is executed with the aid of closing the king on the floor and using a queen to begin the concluding blow. This rook can also be a bishop or Queen.

Damiano's wife regularly comes by sacrificing a collar in report H, then examines the king with the queen in report h, then goes after his wife. Pedro Damiano first posted the Czech agent in 1512. In Damiano's publications, he did not put the white king on the board, which led to his failure to enter many chess databases due to the refusal to accept illegal positions.

The Wife of David and Goliath

David and Goliath's wife is a fashionable way to test. Although David and Goliath's husband can take quite a few forms, they are generally known as the husband in which the infantry is the closing attacking piece, and the enemy's infantry is positioned nearby.

Same Color as Double Bishop

Binary doubling is an ideal way to test. It's like being a wife, but a little easier. The inspector includes the assault on the king, the usage of two bishops, and, consequently, the king is located in the back of a black pedestal that has now not been moved.

Columbofil Colleague

Dovetail's spouse is a preferred way to check. It includes overthrowing the darkish king in the version displayed on the right-hand facet. It doesn't make a difference how the sovereign is upheld; it doesn't make a distinction which of the other pieces is dark as a knight.

Epaulette's Spouse

By way of its genuine definition, epaulet, or Epaulet mate, is an inspection agent in which parallel retreat squares are drawn for a king, occupying parts of it and stopping it from escaping. Epaulette's most everyday spouse consists of the king inside the lower back row, stuck among rooks. The visual resemblance among the rooks and the bulbs, the ornamental portions of the shoulder worn over the army uniforms, gives it the sheet's name.

Greco's Colleague

Greek spouses are a fashionable way to test. This Checkmate agent has been named after the best-regarded catalog of the Italian agent Gioachino Greco. It is finished with the aid of the bishop's use to govern the black king, the use of the black infantry, after which through the queen, to check at the king, transferring him to the chessboard aspect.

The Wife in File H

H-report mate is a way to test. The inspector includes using an alley that attacks the black king, that's supported via the bishop. This frequently takes place after the black king's castles inside the position of maids in his kingdom. White normally enters this position after a chain of sacrifices in case h.

Pair Rook

The pair of rooks consists of a white rook, knight, and infantry in conjunction with a black infantry to limit the black king's escape. The knight protects the rook, and the infantry protects the knight.

The Assignment of the King and the 2 Bishops

The king's venture and the 2 bishops are one of four essential functions alongside the queen's wife, Matt's container, and the bishop and knight. It happens that the king, with bishops, forces the bare king at the nook of the image to pressure a likely wife.

The King and the 2 Knights Have a Project

In a sport of two knights, the king and the 2 knights cannot force an empty king to be arrested. If the empty king is gambling correctly, this last sport has to be drawn. A player makes a mistake most effective if the participant with the empty king is wrong or has already been inside the board's corner.

Lolly's Neighbor

Lolli's wife is a fashionable manner to check. The summary consists of the infiltration of Black's fiancé's position using his leg and queen.

The queen normally arrives in rectangular h6, the usage of the sacrifices in report h, dubbed after Giambattista Lolli.

A Colleague of Max Lange

Max Lange's spouse is a general manner to test. The Czech officer is appointed Max Lange. It is done by the use of the bishop and queen to manipulate the king.

Murphy's Mate

Murphy's spouse is a well-known manner to check. Named after Paul Murphy, this is achieved by the use of a bishop to assault the black king and a rook and a black and white pedestrian to fasten him up. In many ways, he's very much like Corner's wife.

Opera Colleague

Mate Opera is a widespread manner to check. It works through attacking the king within the returned with a rook using a bishop to protect him. A pedestal or other piece apart from the Knight of the Enemy King is used to restrict his movement.

This teammate became named the Opera after the interpretation of Paul Morphy in 1858 in a Paris opera against Dunk Carl de Brunswick and Count Isouard.

Comrade Pillsbury

Pillsbury's wife is a preferred verifier, named after Harry Nelson Pillsbury. As shown on the right, it works with the aid of attacking the king or a pier or bishop. The king can be in g8 or h8 during checkmate.

The Spouse of the Queen

The queen is one of 4 vital missions along with Boxing, King and two Bishops, and Ismail and Knight.

It happens when the party with the queen and king forces the naked queen to the brink or corner of the council. The queen completely examines the naked king, and the pleasant king supports her.

Reti's Mate

Reti marriage is a popular way to test. The Czech officer is known as Richard Reti. Do this via grabbing the enemy king with four portions, which are inside the flying fields, after which attacking him with a bishop who's covered by a rook or a queen.

Colleague Mate

Intimate pairing is a well-known way to test. It occurs that a knight controls the kingdom, which is suppressed (besieged) by its thick portions, and he has nowhere to move, and there is virtually no manner to overcome the knight.

The Neighbor's Sleep

Suffocation is a trendy way of checking. It is performed using the knights to assault the rival king and the bishop to restrict the king's getaway routes.

Swallow's Tail

Swallow's tail, also referred to as Guéridon's wife, is a standard manner to check. It works via attacking the enemy king with a queen included using a rook. The rooks of the enemy king block his escape device. He is very just like Epaulette's spouse.

Chapter 8:

TACTICS

In this chapter, we will be discussing the following basic chess tactics and how they can be used to make your game better:

- Battery Attack

- Discovered Attack

- Discovered Check

- Fork Attack

- Pin Attack

- Skewer Attack

There are many more tactics in chess, but to understand and learn the more complex chess tactics, you will need to know these basic tactics, and these tactics will be taught to you with the help of simple and comprehensible animated diagrams. Now let us take a look at the aforementioned basic chess tactics.

Battery Attack

Battery attack is of a two-kind attack, which comprises of Queen along with Bishop or Rook. In the first kind of attack, the Queen and the Bishop are placed side by side on the Diagonals. In the second kind, the queen is with the rook on the Straights or Ranks or Files.

As the strength of a household battery is increased when an extra cell is added. Likewise, this tactic aims to strengthen the army attack with extra pieces.

Queen and Bishop's Battery

The Diagonals are made use of for this kind of battery. The Bishop is employed as it has greater reach. But whatever the tactic is, only the board positioning will allow the player to take the calculated risk required for this kind of attack. The position of the board is explained with the diagram below for a better understanding.

Queen and Rook's Battery

The Rank or File is made use of for this kind of battery attack where Queen and Rook are employed to add power. It is recommended to make the desired moves with the Rook rather than the Queen, in spite of it being the chief of the battery attack.

Cross roles

Queen and 2x Rooks - Battery

A battery attack with a Queen along with 2 Rooks is considered a powerful, commanding attack, which will give you an advantage over your opponent.

Alexander Alekhine applied such an attack where the Queen and two Rooks on the file move towards the rival when he plays Chess's game. Hence, Alekhine's gun became another name for this attack.

Cross rc. cs

2x Rooks- Battery

Without a Queen, only 2 Rooks on the Ranks or Files can form a battery attack, which can control the board. It is very effective despite being a weaker battery attack compared to the 3 kinds of attacks, as mentioned earlier. But only the game situation can determine the level of effectiveness of such an attack.

Chess skills

Discovered Attack

The two different units of the two opposing players are against each other, but the King of either player is not attacked.

One unit comes into play when the other unit is pulled out of the way. Only then can the unit attack the opponent, such as in the case of the discovered unit.

From the image below, we can understand that Bishop is the uncovered unit or can be called a discovered unit in this scenario.

Cross rcl cs

Discovered Check

Unlike Discovered Attack, in Discovered Check, the King is in danger. The discovered unit attacks the enemy King in this case.

Since the black should save the King according to the diagram. The discovered unit has actually enforced a Check that leads to the Black Queen's sacrifice to save the King. At the same time, when the white Bishop checks the King, the Queen is under the radar of the White Knight.

Chess rules

Fork Attack

In this case, a single unit has the capacity to attack two rival units in one move.

Two Chess Tactics such as Relative Fork and Absolute Fork are explained below with images:

Cross rocks

Relative Fork Attack

The Relative Fork Attack is basically an attack made by one unit on two or more pieces of the opponent in a single tactic that excludes the rival King. It is up to the opponent to decide which piece he wants to rescue and which piece will face the attack. The following diagram shows how a single move of the White's Queen can put the Rook and the Knight of the Black in danger.

Absolute Fork Attack

In the case of Absolute Fork Attack, the King of the enemy is attacked along with another piece or pawn of the opponent in a single move. Since the opponent should save King as the King is checked and leave another piece in danger.

The image shows that the white Queen can attack the Black King and the Rook at the same time.

Cross roles

Pin Attack

This attack comes into play when a lesser important piece or pawn is ahead of an important piece.

There are two types of Pin Attack in the form of Relative and Absolute Pin Attack.

Relative Pin Attack

The less important pawn or piece is attacked if it is before an important key piece, and since it is a relative attack, the important piece is not the King of the rival player.

The White Knight, in this case, is the pinned unit. Such a unit's movement may disturb the formation to safeguard more valuable pieces and put such pieces in danger.

Chess rules

Absolute Pin Attack

As the attack is absolute, the King is in danger. The pinned unit cannot move, as the King's protection is a prime cause of the game. If such a piece tries to move, it is illegal against the rules of Chess where voluntary Check is impossible.

In this scenario, the black Queen should be pinned to the black King due to the white Rook.

Cross roles

Skewer Attack

The identification of an attack is done through the presence of an important piece before a lesser important piece or pawn.

The Relative and Absolute Skewer Attacks are discussed briefly below.

Relative Skewer Attack

The attack is launched on a valuable unit with the view of capturing the lesser valuable unit just behind the valuable unit.

This attack facilitates the movement of important pieces that hindered the lesser valuable piece or pawn's attack.

The white Bishop looking to capture the Black Knight should first threaten the black Rook.

Chess rules

Absolute Skewer Attack

The enemy King is attacked with a Check-in order to capture a lesser valuable piece behind the King. When a Check is enforced, the opponent should save the King by moving if impossible to block with a piece. In that situation, the King's movement opens up the chance to attack the pieces just behind the King.

According to the image, the Rook should be exposed to danger in an attempt to save the King from Check. The white Queen would easily capture the Rook once the King is off the way.

Chess strategy is the art of developing a game plan before and during the game and arranging your pieces to accomplish the plan and realize your objectives. This typically involves continuous assessment of board positions and calculations throughout the game.

Beginners who want to advance to the next level should learn to think and analyze like the pros. To start winning games consistently, you should train your mind to emulate the thought processes involved in a game of chess:

- Evaluating positional elements

- Evaluating tactical elements

- Calculation of variations

- Developing winning combinations

- Testing the soundness of combination

Evaluating Positional Elements

Evaluating chess positions involves finding imbalances in positional elements between you and your opponent. When assessing your position, you need to consider the following elements:

Material Value

Comparing your material with that of your opponent is the most basic way of evaluating the position. Having more powerful pieces on your side is generally an advantage that can be exploited to win the game. Each piece has an assigned value, but this value should be assessed in relation to factors such as mobility position, type of position, and coordination. A piece may have varying relevance depending on its position or the phase of the game you're in. A knight, for instance, has similar value as the bishop, but in tight positions in the opening and the middlegame, a knight enjoys an advantage over the bishop. A knight is more effective when placed in the center, where it has wider attacking range. On the other hand, the bishops tend to be stronger in the endgames when the diagonals are open. Similarly, rooks thrive in the endgame when there are open files and ranks.

Space

Space refers to the squares that a player can use safely and are within his attacking range. The player with more space obviously enjoys an advantage as his pieces have more mobility. In addition, he has broader options for implementing his tactical plays.

Control of the Center

The center is the most important area of the board. Control of the center is vital, particularly in the opening going to the middlegame when tactical combinations are carried out in the center squares. Center control gives your pieces more mobility and more options to attack. Most opening plays are aimed at controlling the center.

Initiative

Initiative refers to a player's activity during the game that allows him to dictate a tempo and his style of play. An initiative can turn into a decisive material or positional advantage. The player with the initiative has control over the course of the game.

Development

Development involves the following:

- Moving pieces to squares where they can be most useful

- Occupying and controlling the center squares

- Efficiently holding back, the opponent's development

Opening plays are aimed at gaining the lead in development. An advantage in development can easily translate to a bigger advantage as the player with well-developed pieces can easily implement tactical combinations.

King's Safety

The king's safety is important in every stage of the game. The player whose king is open to attack at any stage is at a disadvantage. You can expect the opponent to exploit the situation and unleash tactical combinations to gain material or possibly score a checkmate. A castled king is safer than an uncastled one. In the opening game, the king needs to be castled to protect it from the opponent's early tricks. However, in the endgame, the king becomes an active piece and begins to attack loose pieces. It can now defend nearby pawns and accompany them to the opponent's back rank for promotion.

Weak Squares and Open Lines

Weak squares are undefended squares that are open for control and occupation by opposing pieces. A weak square, also known as a hole, can be used to gain a positional advantage.

Open lines allow long-range pieces to exert pressure on the center and on the opponent's side. The bishops, rooks, and queens love open lines and are best in the middle and endgames.

Pawn Structure

Pawn structure is a very important element of the position. Because pawns move slowly and deliberately throughout the game, pawn structure is likely to persist for many moves.

A player with connected pawns and passed pawns have the advantage in the pawn structure.

A passed pawn poses a constant threat to the opponent as it is in a good position for promotion to a more powerful piece, usually a queen. The player can advance the pawn majority on one side of the board to create a passed pawn. On the other hand, connected pawns allow each pawn to cover the weak square of the other and enlarge the player's control on the board.

A player is at a disadvantage if he has isolated pawns, backward pawns, or doubled pawns. Isolated pawns are those with no friendly pawn on either side. They are weak because an enemy piece can be easily placed in front without fear of being captured by the pawn. Backward pawns are weak because they are easily stopped or captured by an enemy piece. A backward pawn usually has difficulty moving forward, especially in cases where an enemy pawn has control over its weak square. Doubled pawns are pawns that are placed on the same column. While doubled pawns have defensive advantages, they are more weak than strong because they have difficulty creating a passed pawn.

Evaluating Tactical Elements

Chess tactics are short sequences of moves aimed at gaining an advantage or winning the game. A series of tactical moves is called a combination. Tactical combinations are logical consequences of position. They are not coincidences that magically appear. A player needs to know how to assess tactical elements to be able to calculate if an advantageous combination can be implemented in the succeeding moves. The tactical elements and considerations that should be taken by the player include the following:

King's Safety

When the enemy King's safety is poor, how can you exploit the weak squares around the opponent's king? What type of maneuvers can you use to attack those squares? Look at the enemy King's defensive pieces. Can you decoy or deflect them to leave their King unprotected? Is there a line that can be opened against the enemy King? When the King is still uncastled, it can open a small window for exploitation. You have to move fast, however, to take advantage of the obvious weakness.

Overloaded Pieces

An overloaded piece is a piece that is performing different roles simultaneously. Taking an overloaded piece out of its square can result in an awkward position or undefended piece. Consider if you could exploit overloaded pieces and disrupt the opponent's plans and defense.

Unprotected Pieces

Are there loose or undefended pieces on your opponent's side? Could you make a move that will create loose pieces that are open for capture?

Pinned Pieces

Can you exploit the pin to gain more advantage? Check the board and see if you can create more pins.

Peculiar Piece Placements

Look at how your opponent's chess pieces are arranged and see if there's something oddly familiar about it. Is a back-rank checkmate possible? Are the enemy pieces too concentrated on one side? How about a battery attack aimed at the enemy King?

Calculation of Variations

You usually have 4 to 6 options on your succeeding plays, and it's important to identify your candidate moves for you to come up with the move that's in sync with your plans or objectives at a particular phase of the game. Since you're limited by time and practical constraints, you have to filter your candidate moves and limit your considerations to the most feasible moves. When analyzing variations, you should prioritize the following moves:

- Forcing moves or moves that pressure your opponent to respond immediately — Thee types of moves are likely to divert his attention and have less chances of being scrutinized.

- Moves that have an impact on the implementation of your strategic plans or goals— These are natural moves that help advance your positional goals and help carry out your overall plan. Such moves may include removing a defender, sacrificing a piece, exploiting a weakened square, and creating a passed pawn.

Your experience naturally limits your choice of candidate moves. The more you play chess and practice tactical combinations, the better your intuition becomes. Just remember to put in some creativity when deciding on what moves to prioritize when analyzing.

Developing a Winning Combination

A successful combination is expected to give a clear advantage to a player who made it, and it is usually expressed in terms of checkmate or material gain.

You may use the following tools to achieve combinational objectives:

- Forcing moves such as a check, a sacrifice, decoy, a capture, a deflection, a discovered attack, or a threat that must be urgently addressed.

- Quieter moves, such as waiting moves, pin, interference, pins, and line opening.

Testing the Soundness of Combinations

This part of the thought process requires you to check if your combination is sound. It is important to test your combination, especially if it involves making a heavy sacrifice. You have to assure yourself that the sacrifice will be worth it.

One way to check your combination is by determining if your opponent can avoid or skip the combination's effects. If this is the case, your sacrifice might turn out to be futile.

Another way to test your tactical plan is by visualizing your pieces on the board and imagining how the opponent will respond to your moves. Think of the best moves your opponent can make. Can he capitalize on your targeted position to turn the play to his advantage?

Chapter 9:

TIPS FOR BEGINNERS

The game chess is definitely an addicting game, and a lot of people get fascinated by it. A person requires both skill and strategy in order to succeed in playing this board game. After knowing the components of the game, the basic rules, and other important information about chess, what you need to do is practice in order to improve your chess skills. It does not necessarily require one to be a genius to start playing chess. Here are some friendly tips and suggestions for beginners of chess:

- During your first few matches, you can record the moves you have made. In this way, you can analyze your strengths and weaknesses in every game and see if the same patterns occur in your games. Find out the moves you think were done wrong so that the next time you can improve your game and do better.

- In order to know more strategies and improve your skills in playing, you can study the games of different grandmasters. A lot of this information can easily be found online. You can watch videos and tutorials so that you can gain more insight into the game.

- Do not consider some pieces inferior as compared to the others. It is important to remember that each piece has its own value to your game. Do not directly consider your Pawns as useless. If used properly, they can be very helpful in stepping up your gameplay.

- Also, don't forget to use all the pieces on your board. Do not just keep moving one or two pieces around because it can give you a lot of checks. You need to utilize your whole army and maximize all possible means of winning the game. One mistake that beginners usually commit is the use of only a few of the pieces in the game. Keep your board alive by moving all your pieces during the game.

- The Queen is the most important and versatile piece you have. Try to protect it as much as possible, but if you ever lose it, do not also think that the game is over, and you have no more chance of winning. Some people begin to play carelessly once they lose their Queen. This is a wrong notion because other pieces are still present, and besides, you still have pawns that can possibly be promoted to a new Queen.

- Before making any movements on the board, think about it twice and do not act on impulse. For beginners, your games are not usually under time pressure, so you have the luxury to think about your moves properly in order to avoid mistakes. Analyze the best possible responses you can do with regards to your opponent's move. Also, think about the possible moves your opponent might do to counter your own moves. Constantly keep track of the moves done by both sides so that you can avoid making mistakes.

- Always be alert and maintain focus while playing. During the game, a lot of distractions may be present around. Try to maintain your attention on the game so that you can keep track of the movements on the board. Some people tend to relax and lose focus, which is why they are prone to miss out on the moves done by their opponent. If you keep looking away, you might not notice that your opponent is already building a strategy in order to trap your king.

- Practice makes perfect. In almost anything you do, whether it is a sport or a hobby, you need to continuously practice in order to improve your skills from time to time. The same thing applies to chess. For beginners, it is advisable to practice regularly and have a partner to play along and learn with. Patience is a virtue; that is why you do not get disappointed if you still find it hard to win during your first few matches. After some time, you will find it easy to read your opponent and create your own game strategies as well.

Chapter 10:

COMMON MISTAKES
TO AVOID

When it comes to chess, you need to learn the main errors that players make and then find out how to avoid doing them yourself. Luckily, you've got this chess guide to help you.

Guard against the following chess mistakes:

Failing to Take Charge of the Center

Don't just look at the chessboard and think you are fine because you still have many pieces to play with. You can lose those ones to a competitor who has half the number of your pieces in a short moment if you are disadvantaged at the chessboard center. Wait until you have become a chess guru to let the center be. But before that, failing to control the center can make or break you in a chess competition.

Look at the center as a hill where the king resides. Don't you wish to be the king, viewing your territory and the subjects therein from a vantage point? That is basically what the player controlling the middle part of the chessboard does. It is relatively easy for such a player to move pieces from one part of the board to another without much risk. The opponent, in the meantime, finds almost every move extremely risky as the opponent's pieces in the middle of the chessboard lie in dangerous wait. So, if you are not yet in the top league, aim to dominate the chessboard center and control it.

Leaving Your King Exposed

What, in the name of competition, are you doing, if at any moment you are leaving your king unprotected? It is tempting, of course, to go for gambits; those opportunities you get to sacrifice a piece or two of your own in order to secure a strategic position, but if in chasing gambits you expose your king, then you are missing the basics. In some African cultures, they call it losing four as you make a dash for two. In chess, you are still in the game until you lose your king. What else could possibly be as important as protecting him? Failure to carefully protect your king very often leads to an embarrassingly early checkmate.

Failure to Develop Your Chess Pieces

Have you watched some people as they begin a game of chess, and one of them seems to mark time just around the starting rows—moving the Queen here and the pawn there and then bringing the Queen back and so on? Some novices try to apply some advanced tactics often shown on videos, and in their view, they are lying in wait for an opportune moment to strike heavy on the opponent's particular piece, often one of the strong ones. But then what, as a novice, you fail to understand is that your opponent has eyes and a tactical mind too. And so, very likely, they can read your plan as you joke around.

To be forewarned is to be forearmed. So, now that your opponent has seen right through your devious mind, do you expect them to leave any loophole, any piece unprotected? In short, your opponent continues to develop their pieces as they keep the others safe, and by the time you realize that the chance you are timing to capture your opponent's Queen or Bishop or whatever other big piece is not forthcoming, it will be an uphill task to begin developing your pieces. Your opponent will have occupied all the strategic locations and will be in full control of the chessboard's middle part.

In short, stop allowing your opponent an early lead. If you cannot lead, at least be at par with your opponent. What you need to ask yourself logically is: if you are out to fight, how would you expect your army to win if you have not allowed any soldiers into the battleground? You need to develop your chess pieces from the word, *go*. That way, you will have great mobility for your pieces, and you can easily enjoy a dynamic play. Besides, when you have developed your pieces well and thus dominated the chessboard center, you can attack your opponent's pieces more effectively and with less risk.

Experts advise that you just adopt this rule until you become a chess master: Develop every piece that you touch for your very first six moves. That means getting them from their home position in the 1st and 2nd ranks and advancing them towards the center of the chessboard, and whenever you can, let your move be protective of another piece in the meantime. Soon, you'll be controlling the center of the board. It will not be you on the receiving end, but you are calling the shots.

Copying Your Opponent's Every Move

I don't want you to be ahead of me, so the minute you move my Queen, I also go for mine; and when you move your Bishop, I move mine. Surely, if I'm your opponent and I realize that you are aping my moves, aren't I going to lead you to the gallows? Often when you copycat, you end up hitting a dead end, and before you realize it, you'll be facing a rude checkmate. Of course, it doesn't mean that you are prohibited from making a particular move just because your opponent made a similar move ahead of you; all you need to do is to ensure that you have a good reason to make whatever move that you choose.

Using Your Queen Very Early

So, you imagine you can play around with your Queen and call checkmate in only five moves just because a video on YouTube said so? Think again—fundamentals cannot be ignored without repercussions. Develop your pieces systematically. These other shortcuts that you see online, including the Scholar's mate, cannot do your game any good if you haven't mastered the art of developing your pieces and how to use your domination of the middle area of the chessboard.

Bringing out your Queen early risks an attack on her, and also, as you try to shield her by taking her back and forth, you waste so much time that you get late to develop your other pieces. The result...? As you have already read above, you end up lagging behind in taking charge of the chessboard's middle area. And instead of attacking, you'll find yourself playing defense against your opponent.

Look at the situation below where a novice thought that the Queen would threaten pieces on the opponent's side from the start of the game and so moved the Queen straight to h5. Since the black player isn't dozing, they can move the black knight to f6 in quick protection.

8	Rook	Knight	Bishop	Queen	King	Bishop	Knight	Rook
7	Pawn	Pawn	Pawn	Pawn	Pawn	Pawn	Pawn	Pawn
6						Nf6		
5		Nb5						
4								
3							g3	
2	Pawn	Pawn	Pawn	Pawn	Pawn	Pawn	Pawn	Pawn
1	Rook	Knight	Bishop	Queen	King	Bishop	Knight	Rook
	A	B	C	D	E	F	G	H

Will you have made any progress? Let's say for now, no, because sooner or later, you may find it necessary to retract that Queen from h5 to a more productive place. And yet, you'll have wasted an opportunity to develop another piece with that initial move.

Wasting Tempos

Yes, tempos are not just in music—they are in chess too. Whenever it is your turn to make a move in chess, it is a tempo. So, if you make a move and after your opponent moves, you follow with another move, those are two tempos for you right there. In a situation where you move your Bishop, say twice consecutively, it beats logic because you had no limitation as to how far you could have moved your Bishop in the first instance. So, effectively, the second tempo was a total waste. Taking a practical example, why move your white Bishop in two moves when one is enough to get him on b5, as you can see from the chessboard above?

What's the big deal with many similar moves? Well, it is wastage. In chess, as you can see, pieces and tempos are resources. You need a strong piece or a strategically located piece to threaten your opponent, and you need an opportunity to make a move— the tempo. So, you need to think carefully before you utilize any of the two. You also need to remember that every move you make that does not add real value to your game, or which is so badly made that it amounts to a tempo waste, is also a lost opportunity to develop another piece.

Being Clumsy on the Chessboard

Look—the game of chess is one where you play with caution, not just because you want to be strategic, but also because you want to do what you mean. Someone may wonder, is there a chance of doing what you don't mean, anyway? Yes, there is. You may think long and hard on your next move but then get careless at the last minute when trying to weigh two options.

Touching One of Your Pieces Inadvertently

If you touch one of your chess pieces during your turn to play, you have no choice but to play it even if it isn't the one you had planned to move. Now, it may be that any move you make with that piece at that moment is dangerous, and the piece is bound to be captured, but the rule holds —if you touch it and it's your turn, you've got to move it.

Exception: However, if you don't like the way a particular piece of yours is sitting on the board and you'd like to adjust it, you can do it on one condition: that you declare audibly, j'adoube! Are you wondering what this means? It means I adjust. And yes, you guessed right—it's French.

Touching Your Opponent's Pieces Inadvertently

Again, if you touch it, you've got to move it. If the piece you inadvertently touched happens to belong to your opponent, you must utilize any room there is to capture it, whether the move is going to advance your cause or not. The only time you can get away with it is if there is no opportunity to capture that piece. Otherwise, it doesn't matter if capturing it would jeopardize the piece you use; as a rule stands, if you touch it, you must act on your touch by capturing the piece.

Hastening to Make a Move

Ha! You think expert chess players just happen to be time-wasters? No way! They know that once you make a move, that is, move your chess piece in play, you cannot change your mind. Once made, a chess move is not reversible—you've got to live with the consequences. That's why it's advisable to take your time when it's your turn to play, checking out all the possible moves you could make and evaluating each option's impact.

Do you think a good game of chess would ever end if no player made a wrong move? Simply put, mistakes are part and parcel of a game—and not just chess, but any game. The best you can do is to learn from those mistakes. If you castled late and your king's position was, therefore, jeopardized, you can't afford to repeat that same mistake in another game. And so, over time, you become a better chess player.

CONCLUSION

When it comes to chess, strategy is the name of the game. Throughout the whole game, one is continually evaluating moves, both for their short-term benefits and long-term place within your overall strategy. From the opening to the endgame, the strategic plan is what helps you to beat your opponent, allowing you to create a checkmate.

This game doesn't just provide strategic mental stimulation, it also has a long history dating back to before the 6th century. As a part of the social fabric of many cultures, it has stood the test of time, tying together humanity with a game of strategy.

Over the years, chess has become a game of skill and tactics, with various options, positions, and rules of play. With international tournaments and other opportunities for the best of the best to play each other and test their skills, this truly is a global game of strategy. We have learned how chess is played in three phases and what each piece means in terms of position and ability.

The various opening moves and tactics, along with strong middlegame evaluations and endgame follow-through, can get you to a win. But along the way, you have to use a plan and follow it to the end. No plan when playing chess puts you into a position of weakness with your opponent or a sound plan can put you in a strong position. While you have to react to your opponent's moves, remember they are also attempting to execute their plan to a successful conclusion. To get that checkmate, you just have to execute yours better!

All the best.